COUNCIL *on* FOREIGN RELATIONS

MW01242275

Annual Report

2022

Annual Report
July 1, 2021–June 30, 2022

Council on Foreign Relations

58 East 68th Street
New York, NY 10065
tel 212.434.9400

1777 F Street, NW
Washington, DC 20006
tel 202.509.8400

cfr.org
communications@cfr.org

Officers

David M. Rubenstein, *Chairman*
Blair W. Effron, *Vice Chairman*
Jami Miscik, *Vice Chairman*
Richard Haass, *President*
Keith Olson, *Executive Vice President and Chief Financial Officer*
James M. Lindsay, *Senior Vice President, Director of Studies, and Maurice R. Greenberg Chair*

Nancy D. Bodurtha, *Vice President, Meetings and Membership*
Irina A. Faskianos, *Vice President, National Program and Outreach*
Suzanne Helm, *Vice President, Philanthropy and Corporate Relations*
Jan Mowder Hughes, *Vice President and Chief Human Resources Officer*
Caroline Netchvolodoff, *Vice President, Education*

Shannon K. O'Neil, *Vice President, Deputy Director of Studies, and Nelson and David Rockefeller Senior Fellow for Latin America Studies*
Iva Zoric, *Vice President, Global Communications and Media Relations*
Stephanie Solomon, *Vice President; Chief Revenue Officer, Foreign Affairs*
Jeffrey A. Reinke, *Chief of Staff to the President, Secretary of the Corporation*

Directors

Term Expiring 2023
Kenneth I. Chenault
Laurence D. Fink
Jane Fraser
Stephen Freidheim
Margaret (Peggy) Hamburg
Charles Phillips
Frances Fragos Townsend

Term Expiring 2024
Thad W. Allen
Afsaneh Mashayekhi Beschloss
Blair W. Effron (Vice Chairman)
Jeh Charles Johnson
Meghan L. O'Sullivan
L. Rafael Reif
Daniel H. Yergin

Term Expiring 2025
Nicholas F. Beim
Timothy F. Geithner
Stephen J. Hadley
James Manyika
Jami Miscik (Vice Chairman)
Richard L. Plepler
Ruth Porat

Term Expiring 2026
Tony Coles
Cesar Conde
Nathaniel Fick
William H. McRaven
Janet Napolitano
Deven J. Parekh
Tracey T. Travis

Term Expiring 2027
Margaret Brennan
Sylvia Mathews Burwell
Ash Carter
James P. Gorman
Laurene Powell Jobs
David M. Rubenstein (Chairman)
Fareed Zakaria

Richard Haass, *ex officio*

Officers and Directors, Emeritus & Honorary

Maurice R. Greenberg
Honorary Vice Chairman

Carla A. Hills
Chairman Emeritus

Robert E. Rubin
Chairman Emeritus

Note: *This list of Officers and Directors is current as of July 1, 2022.*

Contents

Mission Statement

The Council on Foreign Relations (CFR) is an independent, nonpartisan membership organization, think tank, and publisher dedicated to being a resource for its members, government officials, business executives, journalists, educators and students, civic and religious leaders, and other interested citizens in order to help them better understand the world and the foreign policy choices facing the United States and other countries.

Founded in 1921, CFR takes no institutional positions on matters of policy. CFR carries out its mission by

- maintaining a diverse membership, including special programs to promote interest and develop expertise in the next generation of foreign policy leaders;

- convening meetings at its headquarters in New York and in Washington, DC, and other cities where senior government officials, members of Congress, global leaders, and prominent thinkers come together with CFR members to discuss and debate major international issues;

- supporting a Studies Program that fosters independent research, enabling CFR scholars to produce articles, reports, and books and hold roundtables that analyze foreign policy issues and make concrete policy recommendations;

- publishing *Foreign Affairs*, the preeminent journal of international affairs and U.S. foreign policy;

- sponsoring Independent Task Forces that produce reports with both findings and policy prescriptions on the most important foreign policy topics; and

- providing up-to-date information and analysis about world events and American foreign policy on its website, CFR.org.

Letter From the Chair

Chairman
David M. Rubenstein

One hundred years ago, the Council on Foreign Relations (CFR) published the first issue of *Foreign Affairs.* For $1.25, someone picking up the issue in September 1922 could read the lead article by Nobel laureate and former Secretary of State Elihu Root, which argued that the United States had become a world power, and as a result the general population in the country needed to be better informed about international affairs: the very mission of CFR. Another notable author in that first issue was John Foster Dulles, then a financial expert attached to the American Commission to Negotiate Peace, who wrote about Allied debt following World War I. Some thirty years later, he would serve as this country's secretary of state.

Largely a result of the efforts of Edwin Gay, then secretary and treasurer of CFR, the magazine's mission was initially to "guide American public opinion" on foreign policy (this has now been amended to "inform" the public opinion). Gay firmly believed that CFR should produce a journal to advance foreign policy discussion. His idea was to have a quarterly journal—rather than a weekly or monthly periodical—to encourage the highest quality of scholarship.

CFR recruited Archibald Cary Coolidge as the magazine's editor; he was joined by Hamilton Fish Armstrong as managing editor.

At a time when almost all foreign policy debate occurred behind closed doors, *Foreign Affairs* magazine allowed foreign policy specialists to share their analysis with the public. The magazine rapidly established itself as *the* venue for public debate on the subject. It shaped discussions, making sure to tackle the big issues of the day authoritatively. Coolidge and Armstrong sought writers who were competent and well informed, and who championed differences of opinion. In those early days, the magazine published articles by a remarkably diverse group of authors, from W. E. B. Du Bois and Leon Trotsky to Dorothy Thompson and C. C. Wu.

Armstrong became editor upon Coolidge's death in 1928 and went on to become the longest-serving editor of the magazine, guiding it (and often CFR) for much of the next fifty years. Under Armstrong, the journal rose to its greatest prominence after World War II when foreign policy became an integral component of American politics. A seminal piece during this time was the famous article initially attributed to

Vice Chairman
Blair W. Effron

Vice Chairman
Jami Miscik

"X," which was in fact authored by State Department Russia specialist George F. Kennan. The article, "The Sources of Soviet Conduct," laid the groundwork for the doctrine of containment that informed U.S. foreign policy for the four decades of the Cold War.

Although *Foreign Affairs* enjoyed its position as the premier destination for foreign policy discourse, it eventually needed to adapt. While CFR faced internal strife during the Vietnam War, *Foreign Affairs* published numerous articles that dissected the war from different angles. But the magazine was not without its own conflict, with some CFR members expressing outrage when William Bundy, an advisor to the John F. Kennedy and Lyndon B. Johnson administrations on the Vietnam War, replaced Armstrong as editor. Even more concerning for *Foreign Affairs* was the rise of competitors, a changing media landscape, and criticism that its writing was too often predictable and difficult to read.

Subsequent editors worked diligently to modernize the magazine to preserve what was best yet introduce change where needed. When William Hyland and his managing editor, Peter Grose, took over stewardship of the magazine in 1984, they worked to make the magazine more accessible to general readers. That endeavor was carried on by James Hoge Jr. and his managing editor, a young man named Fareed Zakaria who now serves on CFR's Board of Directors with me. Hoge and Zakaria, who took over in 1992, instituted major changes that helped revive the magazine: they introduced article summaries, added a comments section, expanded book reviews, and reduced the typical length for essays from eight-to-twelve thousand to four-to-five thousand words. They were also instrumental in getting Samuel Huntington to publish "The Clash of Civilizations?" in the magazine, which shaped the post–Cold War debate and became the most cited, reprinted, and translated piece in the magazine's history.

When Gideon Rose became editor just over a decade ago, he carried on the legacy of adapting the magazine to the day, focusing on its online presence, and in the process updating it from being merely a mirror of the print magazine to a multifaceted website with content and an identity of its own. As part of that process, he pioneered short, online-only pieces, nearly doubling the content published.

Stewardship of the magazine is now in the capable hands of Daniel Kurtz-Phelan, who previously served as executive editor and is editing the magazine as it begins its second century. Kurtz-Phelan has already expanded the magazine's work on the digital front, publishing more frequent and ambitious articles online and launching other digital products, including a podcast and a virtual event series. Meanwhile *Foreign Affairs* itself is more authoritative than ever, publishing multiple pieces on subjects ranging from Russia and China to energy, climate change, and infectious disease that are defining the foreign policy debate in the United States and beyond.

Given the ever-changing media and geopolitical landscape, the magazine will continue to be adaptive while maintaining its authority. It will continue to publish articles that present original, authoritative ideas on major policy issues. The goal will also be to take that ambition and apply it to an expanding suite of products, including podcasts and newsletters. Content in all of these forms will combine authoritativeness and accessibility and, when relevant, offer policy recommendations rather than just criticisms of current policies. Looking forward, we expect the print edition will remain a core part of the magazine. But the digital experience of readers will receive equal attention. The website (ForeignAffairs.com) will be agile and responsive.

My thanks go to Dan and to Chief Revenue Officer Stephanie Solomon, who handles the business side of the magazine, including printing and logistics, subscriber management, and advertising, for their dedication and work on the magazine as it prepares to celebrate this centennial milestone. In the past year, *Foreign Affairs* has reached records for both revenue and circulation, which is now 217,000 per issue. This all comes on the heels of CFR's own centennial. As the rest of this report underscores, CFR has weathered the challenge of the pandemic and begun the first year of its second century as productive as ever. It continues to be led by Richard Haass with equal parts vision and professionalism. Many thanks as well go to CFR staff, my fellow members of the Board of Directors, and CFR's membership. I am honored to be its chairman as we approach the new year.

President's Message

President
Richard N. Haass

From its inception in 1921, the Council on Foreign Relations has endeavored to be a resource for its members and others who regularly participate in this country's foreign policy conversation: individuals serving in the executive branch, Congress, and the military, as well as journalists, business leaders, academics, and those with a professional or personal interest in international relations and the U.S. role in the world.

This focus continues to dominate the institution's work as it enters its second century. But starting about a decade ago, the Council added a new mission: to be a resource for people mostly unfamiliar with international issues and foreign policy. Motivating this change was the Jeffersonian concept that democracy rests on a foundation of informed citizens and that, in the twenty-first century, being informed requires understanding how the world affects this and every country and person on the planet, and how foreign policy choices in turn affect the world.

This new mission has become a priority for us in a number of ways. First, the Council's Education Department produces three products widely available online and free of charge. Our most recent offering, *Convene the Council*, was designed in partnership with iCivics, the leading civics education content provider, to inspire students as young as twelve to think about foreign policy and why it matters. Players use their critical thinking skills in this educational video game as they navigate scenarios that reveal how foreign and domestic policy are intertwined and how decisions made in one corner of the world can affect all people. *Convene the Council* is one of iCivics' most successful games, one that has been played an average of more than one hundred thousand times per month since its debut in early 2022.

Next is World101, an award-winning curriculum developed in partnership with CFR experts and designed for learners with little or no knowledge of international relations and foreign policy. Lessons on the World101 platform offer jargon-free language and instructor-designed teaching resources, and can be used individually or together to form tailored courses of study. They are broken into five distinct units: globalization, the world's regions, how the world works, history, and basics of foreign policy. The units are made up of more than five hundred pieces of content, including maps, graphs, interviews, text, and videos. Since its launch in December 2019, approximately two million users have visited World101.

The third product, Model Diplomacy, is a simulation program that invites high school, college, and graduate students to step into the shoes of decision-makers on the National Security Council and the UN Security Council to debate the most pressing global issues. Instructors in classrooms in more than 120 countries have drawn on dozens of full-length case studies, an expanding library of short-form scenarios covering current and historical events, and exclusive video content featuring commentary from foreign policy experts to teach students critical thinking, persuasive writing, and collaborative problem-solving as they consider complex international issues.

These resources form the basis of a global civics education, introducing students from middle school all the way through graduate school to the fundamentals of foreign policy and international relations. The goal is to promote global literacy: the knowledge, skills, and perspectives that individuals everywhere need to help them make sense of the world around them, to fulfill their obligations as citizens, and to realize their potential as individuals.

There is as well what we call outreach—offerings made available to diverse communities around the country that go beyond traditional foreign policy circles. Specifically, the Council serves as a resource for four distinct constituencies: educators and students, religious and congregational leaders, state and local officials, and journalists working at regional papers, local broadcast news stations, and digital-first outlets. For each of these groups, we provide dedicated programming that features CFR fellows and other foreign policy experts, disseminate CFR's wide-ranging publications, and participate in related professional gatherings. These constituencies have more influence over the direction of public policy than is often realized and are integral to American society. Additionally, we reach out directly to the general public in this country and around the world through our Home and Abroad public forum series, which is built around events that explore issues at the nexus of U.S. domestic and foreign policy. The most recent forum on the war in Ukraine garnered an audience of 2,400 participants from 61 countries—making it one of our best-attended virtual events. The appetite for a dependable, authoritative, nonpartisan source of information on issues of global importance is clear.

Next is what we do on our award-winning website, CFR.org. The Council's Digital team creates "explainer" content on many platforms, with a focus on "Backgrounders"—pieces on the order of two thousand words that provide the basic facts, history, and analysis of the most important topics in straightforward language complemented by maps, charts, and graphs. Data suggests that CFR.org's core audience comes to the site for context and clarity about unfolding events. Not surprisingly, Backgrounders have become the website's most popular content. In addition, there is a growing range of products including a daily morning newsletter, briefs pegged to breaking news, a growing suite of podcasts, and short (two-minute) explainer videos tailored for distribution on social media, data visualization, and photo essays. Record growth in traffic across all platforms in the past two years shows interest in such resources is increasing. In a digital landscape where biased coverage, misinformation, and disinformation are all too common, CFR.org is committed to offering a steady stream of trustworthy, credible, nonpartisan coverage.

Another way the Council reaches the broader public is through podcasts. The offerings include weekly news-driven podcasts such as *The President's Inbox* and *The World Next Week*; special series such as *Nine Questions for the World*, which in connection with the Council's centennial featured nine extraordinary thinkers exploring the fundamental questions for the next century; a newly launched podcast from the editors of *Foreign Affairs*; and *Why It Matters*, which uses interviews and narratives to explain how critical foreign policy issues have an impact on people and this country and why citizens should learn more about them.

Last but hardly least is all we do to encourage younger citizens to increase their knowledge of the world through direct experience. CFR's paid internship program provides an opportunity for students from around the country to gain practical experience and participate in professional development training as a foundation for future work in the foreign policy field. More than 120 interns join us each year. Junior staff, who are mostly recent college graduates or holders of master's degrees, also support CFR's substantive work and participate in meetings and training akin to the interns. The annual Conference on Diversity in International Affairs brings together more than three hundred young people from communities underrepresented in the field of foreign policy to broaden their knowledge and encourage them to consider pursuing future work on international issues; more than five thousand have participated in the past decade. CFR participates in career fairs at colleges and universities nationwide to raise awareness about professional opportunities. We host substantive briefings at CFR for postsecondary and graduate students and partner with Global Kids, an organization that develops youth leaders at the high school level from underserved communities through global education and leadership development.

The net result is a CFR that is both familiar and different, traditional and innovative. We continue to be the preeminent venue in the United States and arguably the world for generating and discussing the most important ideas and policy proposals, a mission central to our meetings, *Foreign Affairs*, and the work of our fellows. We are also becoming a major provider of educational materials and services to a broader public. Both missions are now central to who we are and what we do. The objective has been and remains to preserve what is best about this institution founded more than a century ago—but also to introduce new roles and activities that meet the challenges and opportunities of the present. We are committed to doing just that.

Richard Haass
President

2022 Highlights

The COVID-19 pandemic persisted over the past year, but the Council on Foreign Relations continued to rise to the challenge and adapt to the circumstances with a gradual return to in-person activities as the year progressed. These highlights reflect a year that included both virtual operations and a hybrid return to the office for both staff and members. Celebrations of CFR's 2021 centennial were finally held in person at receptions in May in New York and Washington, DC, as was the National Conference in June for the first time since 2019.

Meetings

The Council on Foreign Relations provides a nonpartisan forum for thoughtful and informed foreign policy debate, drawing leaders and experts in government, business, the media, and academia for discussions with members on critical issues in foreign policy and international relations.

The Council began hosting hybrid meetings in September starting with the opening of the UN General Assembly—traditionally the busiest time of year for CFR in New York. CFR hosted a number of heads of state and foreign ministers for hybrid events with a limited number of members in attendance and many more online. Heads of state included Taoiseach of Ireland Micheal Martin, President of Iraq Barham Salih, Chancellor Sebastian Kurz of Austria, and the foreign ministers of Egypt, Pakistan, Qatar, Saudi Arabia, South Africa, and South Korea.

Other foreign officials who over the course of the year spoke to members virtually or in person in New York or Washington, DC, include President of Colombia Ivan Duque, Leader of the Opposition in Belarus Sviatlana Tsikhanouskaya, Sinn Fein leader Mary Lou McDonald, Foreign Minister Simon Conveney of Ireland, Prime Minister Lee Hsien Loong of Singapore, former Ukrainian President Petro Poroshenko, and former UK Foreign Secretary and current CEO of the International Rescue Committee David Miliband.

Among the current and former U.S. officials who spoke at CFR were a number of Joe Biden administration officials, including Secretary of Health and Human Services Xavier Becerra, Director of the National Economic Council Brian Deese, Director of National Intelligence Avril Haines, Pentagon Spokesperson John Kirby, Surgeon General Vivek Murthy, Chair of the Council of Economic Advisors and former CFR board member Cecilia Rouse at the keynote session for this year's Stephen C. Freidheim Symposium on Global Economics, National Security Advisor Jake Sullivan, and Centers for Disease Control and Prevention Director Rochelle Walensky. Other U.S. leaders who spoke to members include Representatives Mike McCaul (R-TX), Adam Schiff (D-CA), and Adam Smith (D-WA) and Senators Ben Cardin (D-MD), Bill Cassidy (R-LA), and Ed Markey (D-MA). CFR also held a panel on digital assets with two National Security officials: Anne Neuberger, deputy national security advisor for cyber and emerging technology, and Daleep Singh, deputy national security advisor for international economics.

During 2021, the Council continued the centennial speaker series The Twenty-First-Century World: Big Challenges and Big Ideas, which featured leading thinkers tackling issues that will define this century. Sessions addressed climate change, the role of government and markets, comparative demographic trends and their implications, biotechnology's potential and risks, China, and artificial intelligence. Speakers included Nicholas Stern, chairman of the London School of Economics and Political Science's Grantham Research Institute on Climate Change and the Environment; Minouche Shafik, director of the London School of Economics and Political Science and former deputy governor of the Bank of England; Nicholas Eberstadt, Henry Wendt chair in political economy at the American Enterprise Institute; Michelle McMurry-Heath, president and chief executive officer of the Biotechnology Innovation Organization; Elizabeth Perry, Henry Rosovsky professor of government at Harvard University; and Fei-Fei Li, Denning family codirector of the Stanford Institute of Human-Centered Artificial Intelligence. For the final session, CFR President Richard Haass joined presider Fareed Zakaria to discuss world order. The nine sessions of the series were also released as a podcast, *Nine Questions for the World*.

Top: *Representative of the United States to the United Nations Linda Thomas-Greenfield discusses her career and vision for the future of American diplomacy and U.S. priorities at the United Nations.*

Bottom: *Moderator Margaret Brennan and Former National Security Advisors Condoleezza Rice, Thomas E. Donilon, and Robert C. O'Brien discuss U.S. policy toward Eastern Europe, NATO expansion, and arms control.*

CFR hosted a variety of other meeting series, including Renewing America, which looks at the domestic underpinnings of U.S. foreign policy. Panels in that series included discussions on U.S. trade policy, countering white supremacy, the digital divide, power-grid resilience, political polarization, and public health. In May, CFR hosted a meeting with the six service chiefs (including the commander of the U.S. Space Force), who spoke to members from Washington, DC, as part of the Robert B. McKeon Endowed Series on Military Strategy and Leadership. The Lessons From History series examined the significance of President Richard Nixon's trip to China and its influence on U.S. foreign policy, and how U.S.-China relations have fared in the fifty years since the visit. CFR also hosted a meeting as part of the World Economic Update series, presided over by CFR Senior Fellow Sebastian Mallaby, and a meeting with Kathy Warden of Northrop Grumman as part of the CEO Speaker series. In the C. Peter McColough Series on International Economics, members heard from Governor of the Bank of Canada Tiff Macklem, former U.S. Secretary of the Treasury Lawrence Summers, Martin Wolf of the *Financial Times*, Governor of the Bank of Japan Haruhiko Kuroda, and Federal Reserve Bank of St. Louis CEO and President James Bullard. The John B. Hurford Memorial Lecture featured Ray Dalio of Bridgewater Associates. This year's International Affairs Fellowship (IAF) program conference consisted of a keynote discussion with U.S. Agency for International Development (USAID) Administrator Samantha Power followed by six sessions throughout the summer featuring recent IAF participants. The conference allowed participants to showcase the work they focused on during their time in the program.

The Stephen M. Kellen Term Member Program, which provides five-year memberships for people age thirty to thirty-six, had its twenty-sixth annual conference in November 2021. The conference included an in-person keynote conversation with Representative of the United States to the United Nations Linda Thomas-Greenfield and discussions on threats to democracy, climate change, cybersecurity, U.S.-China relations, and the future of Afghanistan. Term members had numerous other programs over the past year and along with younger life members had the opportunity to hear Thad Allen, Michelle Howard, and Richard Plepler reflect on their careers as part of the Lessons Learned series.

In May, CFR convened the tenth annual Conference on Diversity in International Affairs. The hybrid event, a collaborative effort by CFR, the Global Access Pipeline, and the International Career Advancement Program, featured a keynote by CFR's Steven A. Tananbaum Distinguished Fellow for International Economics Roger W. Ferguson Jr. The conference, held in Washington, brought together more than three hundred college and graduate students and early-career and seasoned professionals from diverse backgrounds that are historically underrepresented in the field of foreign policy to discuss international issues and increase preparedness for careers in the field.

National Program

The National Program connects the plurality of CFR members who live outside New York and Washington, DC, with CFR and its resources. CFR continued to provide virtual programming this year with interactive roundtables via Zoom and resumed limited in-person programming this spring in cities across the country, with events in Atlanta, Austin, Boston, Chicago, Dallas, Los Angeles, Miami, San Francisco, and Seattle, as well as London. The switch to first virtual and now mostly hybrid events during the pandemic has provided CFR's National members with more access to CFR events than ever before.

In December 2021, CFR convened the seventh annual National Symposium in Menlo Park, California, which was CFR's first large-scale hybrid event since the start of the pandemic. Over two hundred members participated, split evenly between in-person and virtual attendance. The symposium included conversations on U.S.-China-Taiwan relations, climate change, and cybersecurity.

In June 2022, CFR hosted the twenty-seventh annual National Conference, which was the first in person in three years and kicked off with a panel on U.S. national security with board members William H. McRaven, Jami Miscik, and Frances Fragos Townsend, moderated by Richard Haass. The conference also included a panel with Glenn Hubbard and Robert E. Rubin, moderated by Gillian Tett, which discussed the U.S. economic outlook, including inflation, the role of the Federal Reserve, and the possibility of a recession. Additional panels discussed geopolitics of energy, Russia and the future of the West, supply-chain strategy, China on the global stage, and governance of global commons.

Founder and Chief Executive Officer of Uncharted Jessica O. Matthews and Senior Fellow Alice C. Hill discuss the role of power delivery systems in creating equitable energy use at the National Symposium.

Top: *Senior Manager of Policy for the Information Technology Industry Council Alexa Lee and Senior Fellow Jennifer Hillman participate in the "Triangle Tensions: China, Taiwan, and the United States" panel at the National Symposium.*

Bottom: *Executive Director and CEO of NAFSA Esther Brimmer, Deputy Assistant to the President and Executive Secretary for the National Space Council Chirag Parikh, and Senior Fellow at the Polar Institute of the Woodrow Wilson International Center for Scholars Evan T. Bloom close out the National Conference with the "New Frontiers in Foreign Policy" panel.*

Corporate Program

CFR's Corporate Program provides member companies from across the globe access to CFR experts, research, and meetings to help them better understand the international issues that affect their businesses. This year, the program held roundtables on standardizing environmental, social, and governance (ESG) metrics, central bank digital currencies, building resilience into supply chains, Russia's economy following the invasion of Ukraine, and the evolution of the energy sector. Other meetings covered China's Digital Silk Road, the economics of demographic change, mandatory cyber incident reporting in the private sector, and the possibility of a global corporate minimum tax.

The Corporate Program hosted its first hybrid annual Corporate Conference in 2022, featuring a keynote conversation with Nasdaq President and CEO Adena Friedman as well as sessions on geopolitical risk, the global economy, and climate change. CFR hosted its fourth annual CEO Summit in June, bringing together nearly twenty leading executives for a candid discussion on many of the economic, geopolitical, and societal factors affecting the private sector.

President and Chief Executive Officer of Nasdaq Adena Friedman and CFR Board of Directors Chairman David M. Rubenstein take a question from the audience in the opening session of the seventeenth annual Corporate Conference.

The David Rockefeller Studies Program

The Studies Program, CFR's think tank, analyzes pressing global challenges and offers recommendations for policymakers in the United States and elsewhere. CFR's research aims to be more policy relevant than that of most universities and more rigorous than what many advocacy groups produce.

CFR experts published six books this year. Rachel B. Vogelstein and Meighan Stone's book, *Awakening: #MeToo and the Global Fight for Women's Rights*, chronicles the remarkable global effects of the #MeToo movement. In *The Fight for Climate After COVID-19*, Senior Fellow Alice C. Hill draws on the lessons and parallels from the COVID-19 pandemic to offer pragmatic strategies to mitigate the devastating effects of climate change and to secure a more prosperous future. In *Master of the Game: Henry Kissinger and the Art of Middle East Diplomacy*, Distinguished Fellow Martin S. Indyk assesses how to—and how not to—succeed at the negotiating table by exploring how Secretary of State Henry A. Kissinger approached his Middle East diplomacy.

Elizabeth Economy's book *The World According to China* explains China's ambitious effort to reshape the current world order to serve its interests and why that will produce a world less free and prosperous for everyone else. In *The Power Law: Venture Capital and the Making of the New Future*, Senior Fellow Sebastian Mallaby provides a comprehensive account of the rise of venture capital and shows why and how the United States' venture-capital model has become the envy of the world and a major source of U.S. economic vibrancy. Senior Fellow Yascha Mounk's *The Great Experiment: Why Diverse Democracies Fall Apart and How They Can Endure* explores one of the greatest challenges of our time—how to make ethnically and religiously diverse democracies work—and offers an optimistic vision of a future in which

Senior Fellow Michelle Gavin discusses the impact of COVID-19 on democracy in Africa, including suspended elections and lockdown measures, during the Darryl G. Behrman Lecture on Africa Policy.

Senior Fellow Luciana Borio and Senior Fellow Ebenezer Obadare participate in a town hall meeting covering the Russian invasion of Ukraine, nuclear negotiations with Iran, recent coups in Africa, tensions with China, and the COVID-19 pandemic.

ethnic and religious divisions matter less than they do now because society has addressed injustices rather than ignored them.

In Council Special Reports, CFR experts provide timely responses to developing crises and contribute to policy debates. CFR published three this year. In *The COVID-19 Pandemic and China's Global Health Leadership*, Senior Fellow Yanzhong Huang assesses China's pursuit of global health leadership amid the COVID-19 pandemic. In *Reflecting Sunlight to Reduce Climate Risk: Priorities for Research and International Cooperation*, Senior Fellow Stewart M. Patrick recommends establishing a national sunlight reflection research program and developing multilateral frameworks for making collective decisions regarding its deployment. In *The Case for a New U.S.-Saudi Strategic Compact*, Senior Fellow Steven A. Cook and Distinguished Fellow Martin Indyk argue that the United States and Saudi Arabia both stand to benefit by renewing their central strategic partnership.

The Center for Preventive Action, under the direction of Senior Fellow Paul B. Stares, published the fourteenth annual *Preventive Priorities Survey* in January. Four hundred foreign policy experts evaluated which conflicts around the world could escalate and harm U.S. interests in 2022. Their top concerns include heightened tensions with Russia over Ukraine, intensifying pressure from

Senior Fellow Sebastian Mallaby, Co-Chief Investment Officer of Sustainability of Bridgewater Associates Karen Karniol-Tambour, and Founder and Chief Executive Officer of Exante Data Jens Nordvig speak at the World Economic Update.

Senior Fellow Yascha Mounk discusses his new book, The Great Experiment, *with CFR President Richard N. Haass.*

China toward Taiwan, a potential confrontation between Iran and Israel, and worsening humanitarian crises in Afghanistan, Haiti, Lebanon, and Venezuela.

The think tank welcomed several new full-time and visiting fellows this year. Michael C. Horowitz joined as a senior fellow for defense technology and innovation; Kenneth I. Juster joined as a distinguished fellow; Zongyuan Zoe Liu joined as a fellow for international political economy; Inu Manak joined as a fellow for trade policy; Carl Minzner joined as a senior fellow for China studies; Ann Norris joined as senior fellow for women and foreign policy; Ebenezer Obadare joined as the Douglas Dillon senior fellow for Africa studies; Brad W. Setser rejoined as the Whitney Shepardson senior fellow; Laura Taylor-Kale joined as a fellow for innovation and economic competitiveness; and Christopher M. Tuttle joined the Studies Program as a senior fellow and director of the Renewing America initiative.

Council of Councils

This year, the Council of Councils, a consortium of twenty-eight leading think tanks from around the world that convenes semiannually to discuss the state of global governance and how to improve it, met virtually in October, December, and March, and in person in June in Washington, DC. This year marked the group's eleventh annual conference, during which discussions spanned a wide range of challenges for multilateral cooperation, including the war in Ukraine, emerging pandemic threats, climate risk, and the fate of democracy.

Education

CFR's educational initiative aims to provide students with the skills and knowledge about the world to prepare them for a wide range of careers and ensure an informed citizenry. Model Diplomacy, CFR's National Security Council simulation program, continued to release new simulations and pop-up cases—short policy scenarios, some tied to current events and others to historical events. Model Diplomacy introduced pop-up cases on Afghanistan and Taiwan and added short-form cases on deforestation in the Amazon and U.S. arctic policy, as well as two series: one on the war in Ukraine and the other a companion to the World101 unit on the tools of foreign policy.

World101—CFR's online modular course that focuses on the fundamental concepts of international relations and foreign policy— reached a major milestone with the release of the fifth and final unit, Foreign Policy. The three modules and twenty-eight lessons making up this unit cover the various approaches to international relations, provide a comprehensive review of the tools available to policymakers, and offer a detailed look at the processes and agencies involved in creating U.S. foreign policy. World101 now has 5 units (on global era issues, regions of the world, how the world works, historical context, and foreign policy) consisting of 27 modules and 407 multimedia lessons.

In March 2022, when many teachers and parents sought high-quality content to help explain and explore the crisis in Ukraine, CFR launched *Convene the Council*, a foreign policy game developed in partnership with iCivics. The new product opened CFR resources to a middle school audience, allowing students as young as twelve (and their instructors and parents) to learn about global affairs. The foreign policy scenarios that compose *Convene the Council*'s simulation program introduce students to the basics of U.S. foreign policy. The gameplay invites users to navigate the difficult balance between foreign and domestic needs and determine a course of action that best supports U.S. interests and values. In the game, students consider how their policy decisions could play out internationally, how the United States could respond, and how decisions made in one corner of the world can—and often do—affect all people.

Educators watch the CFR Education Presentation at the College and University Educators Workshop.

Outreach

Academic Outreach

CFR's Academic Outreach initiative connects educators and students with CFR publications, digital educational products, and programming for teaching and learning about international affairs. The initiative continued its long-standing series for students and professors as well as its series for higher education leaders, administrators, and professors, and held both virtual and in-person conferences and workshops. It also focused on broadening the range of participants through efforts with historically Black and Hispanic colleges and universities and community colleges. In April, CFR held the annual College and University Educators Workshop, with nearly seventy participants attending in person and more than eighty virtually.

Religion and Foreign Policy Program

Since 2006, CFR's Religion and Foreign Policy program has provided a unique nonpartisan forum in which to examine issues at the nexus of religion and U.S. foreign policy. This year the program expanded its coverage with webinars about the legality of religious exemptions to the COVID-19 vaccine and explored the United States' human rights credibility gap. In May, the program convened the Religion and Foreign Policy Workshop as a hybrid event with more than seventy members of the religion community gathered in person and more than one hundred online. The program also organized multiple webinars, covering topics from refugee resettlement to the religion dimension of Russia's invasion of Ukraine.

Washington Outreach

CFR's Congress and U.S. Foreign Policy program aims to connect the work of CFR with members of Congress, their staffs, and executive branch officials. The program is an essential source of independent, nonpartisan analysis to inform the direction of U.S. foreign policy.

It also offers a unique forum in which policymakers from both sides of the aisle can come together for all-too-rare reasoned discussions on foreign policy issues.

The program hosts a weekly congressional staff webinar series, a virtual foreign policy roundtable series, and private, on-request consultations with members of Congress and their staffs. This year, the program facilitated briefings and consultation for Congress both virtually and in person, in addition to general outreach and relationship-building meetings with members of Congress and their staffs. Congress continues to turn to CFR for thoughtful analysis of pressing foreign policy issues—including those related to Afghanistan, China, and Russia—and throughout 2022, CFR fellows have briefed members and staff from nearly two hundred offices.

The House and Senate principals meeting series, cohosted with former Senator Tom Daschle and former Congressman Vin Weber, held its second virtual roundtable of the 117th Congress, convening sixteen members of the U.S. House and Senate for a conversation on Russia.

State and Local Outreach

CFR's State and Local Officials initiative connects governors, mayors, state legislators, and city and county leaders with resources on pressing global issues that affect local agendas. This year the initiative launched a series on understanding the Infrastructure and Investment Job Act, with sessions on water; resilient and sustainable infrastructure projects; and race, voting rights, and democracy in the United States. Additionally, the initiative began and deepened relationships with influential organizations such as the National League of Cities, the National Conference of State Legislatures, the National Association of Attorneys General, and the U.S. Conference of Mayors.

Local Journalists Initiative

To elevate conversations on U.S. foreign policy choices and increase civic participation, CFR's Local Journalists initiative helps print, broadcast, and digital native journalists working for regional outlets throughout the United States to draw connections between the local issues they cover and national and international dynamics. CFR continued the conference call and webinar series for those journalists to connect them with experts and provide a forum for sharing best practices. The Local Journalists initiative also held a workshop in person at CFR to introduce journalists to CFR's wealth of free resources and discuss best practices for connecting international events with local issues that affect their audiences.

Home and Abroad Series

In 2021, CFR launched the Home and Abroad public forum series, whose quarterly events educate the general public on issues at the nexus of U.S. domestic and foreign policy that affect the United States' role in the world. More than 750 participants attended the October conversation with CFR's Alice Hill, University of Miami's Katharine Mach, and Stanford University's Arun Majumdar on current and projected climate change, options for reducing emissions, and policies to help communities adapt. More than 2,400 participants from more than 60 countries participated in the March conversation on the Russia-Ukraine crisis that Richard Haass moderated with Ivo H. Daalder, Fiona Hill, and Mary Elise Sarotte—making it the highest-attended virtual event CFR has hosted to date.

CFR Vice President and Deputy Director of Studies Shannon K. O'Neil, W. Bradford Wiley Chair in International Economics at Colgate University Chad Sparber, Charles J. Merriam Distinguished Professor of Law at Arizona State University Angela M. Banks, and Foreign Affairs *Senior Editor Alexandra Starr take questions from the audience during the "Immigration and the Economy" panel at the 2022 Local Journalists Workshop.*

CFR Digital

CFR.org continues to be a leading source of timely analysis on critical foreign policy issues. The website's most popular pieces of content continue to be Backgrounders, which provide authoritative, accessible, and regularly updated primers on hundreds of foreign policy topics from around the globe. In Briefs, which provide succinct rundowns on important developments authored by CFR fellows and the CFR.org editorial team, and Backgrounders produced this year covered topics including the U.S. withdrawal from Afghanistan and Russia's war in Ukraine.

CFR continued to provide comprehensive coverage on the pressing foreign policy issues of the day. The editorial team and fellows collaborated on a package of special coverage related to the twentieth anniversary of the 9/11 attacks, including a topic page containing recent coverage and curated content from the past year at CFR. As the Taliban swept to power amid the U.S. withdrawal from Afghanistan, CFR.org published many articles, Backgrounders, and In Briefs, including a Backgrounder on the Taliban and a popular interactive timeline on the war in Afghanistan. As the world shifted focus to Ukraine following the February 24 invasion,

CFR.org published more than eighty pieces of original content, including Backgrounders, short explainer articles, videos, timelines, conflict trackers, and podcasts. The volume of work produced by CFR scholars and editors was even higher when including articles published by *Foreign Affairs*, Think Global Health, and outside publications.

CFR launched a new digital hub for Renewing America, which contains a wide variety of original content from CFR's scholars and editorial team, including books, reports, blogs, Backgrounders, In Briefs, and events. The hub focuses on nine critical issues including education, energy and climate change, the future of work, immigration, infrastructure, innovation, democracy and political institutions, social justice and equity, and trade and finance. In October, Senior Fellow Benn Steil and analyst Benjamin Della Rocca launched the "Global Trade Tracker" interactive. The tracker charts trends in global trade for 178 countries over the last 30 years and shows how trade plunges during recessions and climbs during recovery. CFR also relaunched two franchises: the "Global Conflict Tracker" and interactive timelines. The "Global Conflict Tracker," which remains one

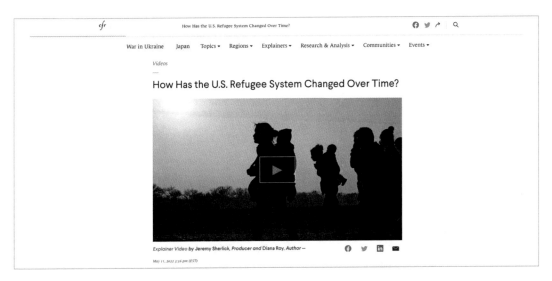

Explainer videos created by the Council's Digital team provide context and clarity for CFR.org's core audience.

of the website's most popular features, benefited from an extensive redesign, with revamped images and easier-to-access news alerts and background information.

Think Global Health, a multicontributor website CFR launched in January 2020 to explore how health challenges are reshaping economies, societies, and everyday lives around the world, has produced more than 500 articles and received more than 2.6 million page views during its first 2 years in operation. Contributors have come from sixty countries. Major news outlets, such as the *Atlantic*, the BBC, the *New York Times*, and the *Washington Post*, have regularly linked to the site's content.

CFR's public newsletters—including the *Daily Brief, Members' Weekly,* and *The World This Week*—continue to attract new subscribers. In addition, CFR maintains a significant presence on social media. CFR institutional social media accounts now have more than half a million followers on Twitter, more than 415,000 on Facebook, more than 235,000 on LinkedIn, and more than 45,000 on Instagram, reflecting steady growth on most channels. The Council's YouTube channel now has nearly 200,000 subscribers. CFR experts have roughly 1.8 million followers on Twitter and 65,000 followers on Facebook.

The CFR.org home page features a timely publication, such as this timeline of Russia's invasion of Ukraine, along with a series of recent stories.

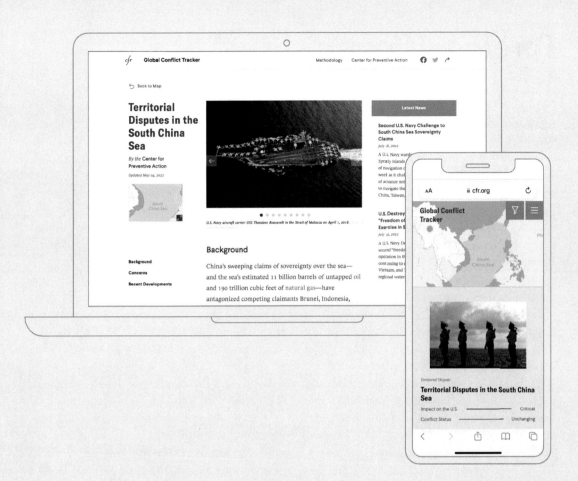

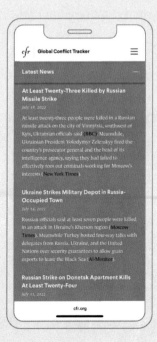

The "Global Conflict Tracker" has been redesigned for ease of reading on desktop and mobile.

Foreign Affairs

Foreign Affairs magazine is celebrating its centennial in 2022 and remains the most thoughtful, read, and influential journal in its field. The magazine complements all else CFR does by providing a space for long-form analysis from a broad pool of expert voices. Each bimonthly print issue includes a lead package on a consequential issue, accompanied by in-depth analysis of other challenges. In addition, ForeignAffairs.com offers authoritative commentary several times a week on the latest foreign policy developments.

Lead packages in the magazine this year explored the rise of China, the legacy of the war on terror, the new Cold War and the future direction of U.S. foreign policy, cyber threats, the Middle East, and the war in Ukraine. The magazine also included essays by Thant Myint-U on deepening state failure in Myanmar, James Manyika and Michael Spence on the future of economic productivity, Elizabeth Economy on Xi Jinping's ambitions, Jason Bordoff and Meghan O'Sullivan on the geopolitics of the green energy transition, Arvind Subramanian on India's economy, Stephen Kotkin on Russian President Vladimir Putin's aims in Ukraine, and Mary Elise Sarotte on the history of NATO expansion.

ForeignAffairs.com has been publishing eight to ten new pieces a week, with highlights including a series by Liana Fix and Michael Kimmage on the possible paths the war in Ukraine will take, Angela Stent on Russia's battle for the Black Sea and the future of navigation, Andrei Kolesnikov on Russian reactions to the war in Ukraine, Steven Levitsky on the future of American democracy, Abhijit Banerjee and Esther Duflo on the pandemic's damage to the developing world, Mohamed Adow on climate change in the developing world, Odd Arne Westad on the China-Russia relationship, Andrea Kendall-Taylor on Putin's future, Yanzhong Huang on China's zero-COVID strategy, and Caitlin Talmadge on AUKUS, the trilateral security agreement among Australia, the United Kingdom, and the United States.

Foreign Affairs is also celebrating its centennial with a variety of initiatives, including a series of events featuring conversations with prominent *Foreign Affairs* authors and influential figures in foreign policy and international affairs; a podcast featuring interviews with authors; and a weekly newsletter and collection featuring notable articles from the past century that includes the weekly circulation of a major piece, the first being George Kennan's 1947 "X" article.

ANTONY BLINKEN
U.S. Secretary of State

DANIEL KURTZ-PHELAN
Editor, Foreign Affairs

U.S. Secretary of State Antony Blinken joined Foreign Affairs *Editor Daniel Kurtz-Phelan for a conversation about the evolution of American foreign policy and the challenges facing the Joe Biden administration in regard to Russia, China, the war in Ukraine, and more.*

Membership

Membership

Since its founding in 1921, the Council on Foreign Relations has grown a membership of more than five thousand prominent leaders in the foreign policy arena, including top government officials, scholars, business executives, journalists, lawyers, and nonprofit professionals. The membership is composed of those residing in the greater New York and Washington, DC, areas, and a plurality based around the United States and abroad.

CFR members enjoy unparalleled access to a nonpartisan forum through which they engage with and gain insight from experts in international affairs. Members have in-person access to world leaders, senior government officials, members of Congress, and prominent thinkers and practitioners in academia, policy, and business, many of whom are members themselves. Convening nearly one thousand events annually, CFR is dedicated to facilitating an intellectual exchange of ideas through expert panel discussions, symposia, town halls, livestreams, and CEO forums exclusively for members. Through exposure to CFR's think tank, publications, briefing materials, and special content on CFR.org and ForeignAffairs.com, members benefit from an expansive collection of unmatched intellectual capital and resources.

The Council seeks quality, diversity, and balance in its membership. Criteria for membership include intellectual achievement and expertise; degree of experience, interest, and current involvement in international affairs; promise of future achievement and service in foreign relations; potential contributions to CFR's work; desire and ability to participate in CFR activities; and standing among peers. New members are elected twice a year by the Board of Directors.

Applying for Membership
Eligibility Requirements

- Membership is restricted to U.S. citizens (native born or naturalized) and permanent residents who have applied to become citizens.

- CFR visiting fellows are prohibited from applying for membership until they have completed their fellowship tenure.

- CFR members are required to fulfill annual dues requirements.

Candidates must submit an online application, complete with a nominating letter from a current CFR member and seconding letters from three to four other individuals.

To apply for membership, visit cfr.org/membership/individual-membership.

Membership Deadlines and Candidate Notification

The two annual membership application deadlines are March 1 and November 1. All membership candidates and their letter writers will receive notification of the election decisions in late June for the March 1 deadline, and in early March for the November 1 deadline.

For More Information

To learn more about the membership application process or for information on nominating a candidate, visit cfr.org/membership or contact Membership at 212.434.9456 or applications@cfr.org.

Stephen M. Kellen Term Member Program

The Stephen M. Kellen Term Member Program, established in 1970 to cultivate the next generation of foreign policy leaders, encourages professionals from diverse backgrounds to engage in a sustained conversation on international affairs and U.S. foreign policy. Each year, a new class of term members between the ages of thirty and thirty-six is elected to serve a fixed five-year term. Term members enjoy a full range of activities, including events with high-profile speakers; an annual Term Member Conference; roundtables; trips to various sites, including military bases, international organizations, and U.S. governmental agencies; and one weeklong study trip abroad every two years.

For more information on the Term Member Program, please visit cfr.org/membership/term-member-program.

Applying for Term Membership
Eligibility Requirements

- Term membership is restricted to U.S. citizens (native born or naturalized) and permanent residents who have applied to become citizens.

- Candidates for term membership must be between the ages of thirty and thirty-six on January 1 of the year in which they apply.

- CFR visiting fellows are prohibited from applying for term membership until they have completed their fellowship tenure.

- Graduate students should generally wait until after the completion of their degree to apply for term membership.

- CFR term members are required to fulfill annual dues requirements.

Term membership candidates must submit an online application, complete with a nominating letter from a current CFR member and seconding letters from two to three other individuals.

To apply for term membership, visit cfr.org/membership/individual-membership.

Term Membership Deadline and Candidate Notification

The annual application deadline for term membership is January 10. All term membership candidates and their letter writers will receive notification of the election decisions in late June.

Profile of the Membership

Between July 2021 and June 2022, CFR membership held steady at 5,172 members. Member records are maintained by CFR at 58 East 68th Street, New York, NY 10065.

Location	Number of Members	Percentage of Membership
National	2,206	43
New York Area	1,426	27
Washington, DC, Area	1,540	30
Total	5,172	100

Industry		
Education	1,052	20
Nonprofit	988	19
Financial Institutions	779	15
Law and Consulting	648	13
Government	444	9
Media and News Services	325	6
Commerce	170	3
Information Technology	163	3
Military	112	2
Medicine and Health Care	57	1
Energy and Power	31	1
Other	403	8
Total	5,172	100

5,172
individual members

New York Area

1,426

Washington, DC, Area

1,540

National

2,206

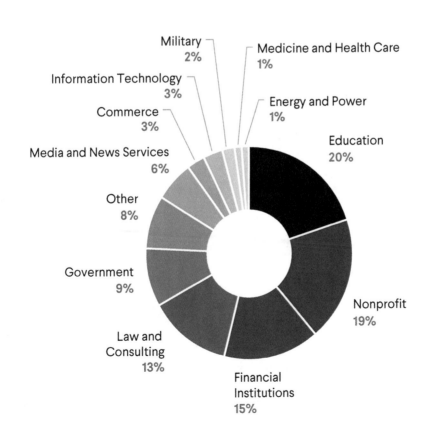

Military 2%

Medicine and Health Care 1%

Information Technology 3%

Commerce 3%

Media and News Services 6%

Other 8%

Government 9%

Law and Consulting 13%

Financial Institutions 15%

Energy and Power 1%

Education 20%

Nonprofit 19%

Corporate Program

Profile of the Corporate Membership

Founded in 1953 with twenty-five corporate members, the Corporate Program has since expanded to include more than 120 companies from various industries and regions of the world. Through CFR's unmatched convening power, the program links private-sector leaders with decision-makers from government, media, nongovernmental organizations, and academia to discuss issues at the intersection of business and foreign policy.

Corporate membership is available at three levels: Founders ($100,000), President's Circle ($75,000), and Affiliates ($40,000). Member companies are offered briefings by in-house experts, a members-only website, CFR resources tailored to the private sector, and roundtables designed specifically for executives. The highlight of the program year is the annual Corporate Conference, which addresses such topics as competitiveness, geopolitical risk, and the global economic outlook. Additionally, the program provides professional development opportunities for individuals on a senior management track through its Corporate Leaders Program, and, for those with fewer than ten years of experience, through its Young Professionals Briefing series.

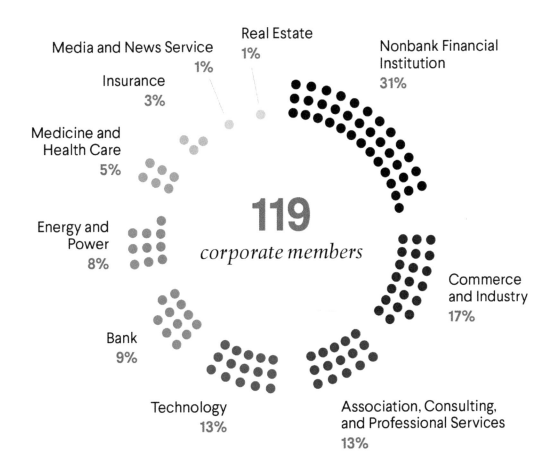

119
corporate members

- Media and News Service 1%
- Real Estate 1%
- Nonbank Financial Institution 31%
- Insurance 3%
- Medicine and Health Care 5%
- Energy and Power 8%
- Bank 9%
- Technology 13%
- Association, Consulting, and Professional Services 13%
- Commerce and Industry 17%

Note: *Percentages do not necessarily total 100 because of rounding.*

Benefits of Corporate Membership

Founders ($100,000+)

All President's Circle and Affiliates benefits plus:

- Four CFR fellow briefings tailored to the company's interests

- Professional development opportunity for four rising executives to participate as "Corporate Leaders" in conjunction with the competitive Stephen M. Kellen Term Member Program

- One rental of the historic Harold Pratt House ballroom and library (based on availability)

- Fifteen *Foreign Affairs* print subscriptions

- One-time cover or premium position advertisement in *Foreign Affairs* and exclusive discounts on digital, sponsored content, and continued print advertising

- Prominent logo placement on the Corporate Program webpage and at the Corporate Conference

President's Circle ($75,000)

All Affiliates benefits plus:

- Invitations for leadership-level executives to attend the Chairman's Circle Dinner and the Annual Dinner with CFR's Board of Directors and Global Board of Advisors

- Opportunities for senior executives to participate in study groups and roundtables led by CFR fellows, and attend exclusive events with noted thinkers and practitioners in government, policy, academia, and the private sector

- Two CFR fellow briefings tailored to the company's interests

- Professional development opportunity for two rising executives to participate as "Corporate Leaders" in conjunction with the competitive Stephen M. Kellen Term Member Program

- Ten *Foreign Affairs* print subscriptions

- One-time full-page advertisement in *Foreign Affairs* and exclusive discounts on digital, sponsored content, and continued print advertising

Affiliates ($40,000)

- Invitations for executives to participate in hundreds of CFR events each year held virtually and/or in New York, Washington, DC, and other major cities in the United States and around the world

- Invitations to rapid-response discussions led by CFR fellows and other experts

- Access to meeting replays, CFR resources tailored to the private sector, and other digital resources, including the member services portal

- Opportunities for senior executives to participate in special meetings and round-tables with CFR's president

- Opportunities for young professionals to participate in special briefings and select meetings

- Invitations for executives to attend the Corporate Conference, CFR's annual summit on geopolitical and geoeconomic issues of interest to the global business community

- One CFR fellow briefing tailored to the company's interests

- Reduced rates for rental of the Harold Pratt House in New York City and 1777 F Street in Washington, DC

- Six *Foreign Affairs* print subscriptions

- Exclusive discounts on additional *Foreign Affairs* subscriptions, advertising, and custom events with editors

- Recognition on CFR's corporate membership roster

Note: Corporate membership dues are 65 percent tax deductible.
For more information, please contact the Corporate Program at corporate@cfr.org or 212.434.9684.

Financial Highlights

Statements of Financial Position

As of June 30, 2022 (with comparative totals for June 30, 2021)

Assets	2022	2021	Change
Cash and cash equivalents	$ 47,595,400	$ 49,786,200	$ (2,190,800)
Accounts receivable, net	2,042,000	1,955,900	86,100
Prepaid expenses	1,310,500	1,181,200	129,300
Grants and contributions receivable, net	8,310,200	13,088,400	(4,778,200)
Contributions receivable for endowment, net	10,071,900	14,443,000	(4,371,100)
Inventory	242,900	167,200	75,700
Investments	544,085,500	589,309,500	(45,224,000)
Land, buildings and building improvements, and equipment, net	60,512,800	62,930,300	(2,417,500)
Total assets	**674,171,200**	**732,861,700**	**(58,690,500)**

Liabilities			
Accounts payable and accrued expenses	9,077,500	8,989,700	87,800
Deferred revenue	7,283,000	6,251,100	1,031,900
Accrued postretirement benefits	3,713,000	4,949,000	(1,236,000)
Interest-rate swap agreement	2,604,200	7,659,100	(5,054,900)
Bonds payable	46,570,000	48,630,000	(2,060,000)
Total liabilities	**69,247,700**	**76,478,900**	**(7,231,200)**

Net assets			
Without donor restrictions	135,316,200	142,857,100	(7,540,900)
With donor restrictions	469,607,300	513,525,700	(43,918,400)
Total net assets	**604,923,500**	**656,382,800**	**(51,459,300)**
Total liabilities and net assets	**$674,171,200**	**$732,861,700**	**$(58,690,500)**

Note: To view the full 2022 Financial Statements, please visit cfr.org/annual-report-2022.

Statement of Activities

For the year ended June 30, 2022

Operating revenue and support	Without donor restrictions	With donor restrictions	Total
Membership dues	$ 8,365,400	$ —	$ 8,365,400
Annual giving	10,680,500	—	10,680,500
Corporate memberships and related income	6,780,700	148,500	6,929,200
Grants and contributions	3,376,100	7,233,400	10,609,500
Foreign Affairs publications	10,797,000	—	10,797,000
Investment return used for current operations	6,930,400	17,209,500	24,139,900
Rental income	1,118,900	—	1,118,900
Miscellaneous	89,200	—	89,200
Net assets released from restrictions	29,136,400	(29,136,400)	—
Total operating revenue and support	**77,274,600**	**(4,545,000)**	**72,729,600**

Operating expenses

Program expenses:			
Studies Program	24,397,000	—	24,397,000
Task Force	416,200	—	416,200
NY Meetings	1,336,700	—	1,336,700
DC programs	1,448,600	—	1,448,600
Special events	630,700	—	630,700
Foreign Affairs publications	11,426,000	—	11,426,000
National Program	1,300,200	—	1,300,200
Outreach Program	1,732,700	—	1,732,700
Term member	414,000	—	414,000
Digital Program	5,766,300	—	5,766,300
Education Program	4,887,100	—	4,887,100
Global Board of Advisors	28,400	—	28,400
Total program expenses	**$53,783,900**	**$ —**	**$53,783,900**

Note: To view the full 2022 Financial Statements, please visit cfr.org/annual-report-2022.

	Without donor restrictions	With donor restrictions	Total
Supporting services			
Fundraising:			
Development	$ 2,274,600	$ —	$ 2,274,600
Corporate Program	1,800,300	—	1,800,300
Total fundraising	**4,074,900**	**–**	**4,074,900**
Management and general	16,722,100	—	16,722,100
Membership	1,911,600	—	1,911,600
Total supporting services	**22,708,600**	**–**	**22,708,600**
Total operating expenses	**76,492,500**	**–**	**76,492,500**
Excess (deficiency) of operating revenue and support over operating expenses and transfers	**782,100**	**(4,545,000)**	**(3,762,900)**
Nonoperating activities			
Investment gain in excess of spending rate	(14,613,900)	(40,989,400)	(55,603,300)
Endowment contributions	—	1,616,000	1,616,000
Change in value of interest-rate swap agreement	5,054,900	—	5,054,900
Other	—	—	—
Postretirement changes other than net periodic costs	1,236,000	—	1,236,000
Transfer from operating to innovation fund for *Foreign Affairs*	—	—	—
Total nonoperating activities	**(8,323,000)**	**(39,373,400)**	**(47,696,400)**
Change in net assets	**(7,540,900)**	**(43,918,400)**	**(51,459,300)**
Net assets, beginning of year	**142,857,100**	**513,525,700**	**656,382,800**
Net assets, end of year	**$135,316,200**	**$469,607,300**	**$604,923,500**

Note: To view the full 2022 Financial Statements, please visit cfr.org/annual-report-2022.

Statement of Activities

For the year ended June 30, 2021

Operating revenue and support	Without donor restrictions	With donor restrictions	Total
Membership dues	$ 8,052,200	$ —	$ 8,052,200
Annual giving	10,605,200	—	10,605,200
Corporate memberships and related income	6,850,000	121,700	6,971,700
Grants and contributions	1,470,500	10,732,500	12,203,000
Foreign Affairs publications	9,298,200	—	9,298,200
Investment return used for current operations	6,895,500	16,098,600	22,994,100
Rental income	151,300	—	151,300
Miscellaneous	73,900	—	73,900
Net assets released from restrictions	27,245,900	(27,245,900)	—
Total operating revenue and support	**70,642,700**	**(293,100)**	**70,349,600**

Operating expenses

Program expenses:			
Studies Program	22,565,700	—	22,565,700
Task Force	446,100	—	446,100
NY Meetings	1,061,600	—	1,061,600
DC programs	1,279,900	—	1,279,900
Special events	600,800	—	600,800
Foreign Affairs	9,772,700	—	9,772,700
National Program	855,400	—	855,400
Outreach Program	1,471,000	—	1,471,000
Term member	351,700	—	351,700
Digital Program	5,524,100	—	5,524,100
Education Program	4,898,700	—	4,898,700
Global Board of Advisors	26,800	—	26,800
Total program expenses	**$48,854,500**	**$ —**	**$48,854,500**

Note: To view the full 2022 Financial Statements, please visit cfr.org/annual-report-2022.

	Without donor restrictions	With donor restrictions	Total
Supporting services			
Fundraising:			
Development	$ 2,113,600	$ —	$ 2,113,600
Corporate Program	1,741,200	—	1,741,200
Total fundraising	**3,854,800**	**—**	**3,854,800**
Management and general	14,747,200	—	14,747,200
Membership	1,654,200	—	1,654,200
Total supporting services	**20,256,200**	**—**	**20,256,200**
Total operating expenses	**69,110,700**	**—**	**69,110,700**
Transfer from operating to innovation fund for *Foreign Affairs*	(1,000,000)	—	(1,000,000)
Excess (deficiency) of operating revenue and support over operating expenses and transfers	**532,000**	**(293,100)**	**238,900**
Nonoperating activities			
Investment gain in excess of spending rate	23,886,400	76,908,300	100,794,700
Endowment contributions	—	7,896,800	7,896,800
Change in value of interest-rate swap agreement	3,259,800	—	3,259,800
Other	(205,000)	(100,000)	(305,000)
Postretirement changes other than net periodic costs	899,000	—	899,000
Transfer from operations to Innovation Fund for *Foreign Affairs*	1,000,000	—	1,000,000
Total nonoperating activities	**28,840,200**	**84,705,100**	**113,545,300**
Change in net assets	**29,372,200**	**84,412,000**	**113,784,200**
Net assets, beginning of year	**113,484,900**	**429,113,700**	**542,598,600**
Net assets, end of year	**$142,857,100**	**$513,525,700**	**$656,382,800**

Note: To view the full 2022 Financial Statements, please visit cfr.org/annual-report-2022.

Credits

Editor: Patricia Lee Dorff
Associate Editor: Cassandra Jensen
Photo Editor: Luke Campopiano
Copy Editor: Glenn Court
Copy Design: Sabine Baumgartner and Dalia Albarran Palma
Production: Dalia Albarran Palma and Gene Crofts
Publications Intern: Chelsea Padilla

Photos
Page 14: Don Pollard
Page 16: Sherman Chu
Page 17: Sherman Chu, Don Pollard
Page 18: Don Pollard
Page 22: Don Pollard
Page 24: Don Pollard

Made in the USA
Middletown, DE
13 November 2022

14860264R00027